Lingo Dingo
and the
French astronaut

Written by Mark Pallis
Illustrated by James Cottell

For my awesome sons Oscar and Felix - MP

For Sophia - JC

LINGO DINGO AND THE FRENCH ASTRONAUT

Story edited by Natascha Biebow, Blue Elephant Storyshaping
First Printing, 2022
ISBN: 978-1-913595-93-7
NeuWestendPress.com

Lingo Dingo
and the
French astronaut

Written by Mark Pallis

Illustrated by James Cottell

NEU WESTEND
— PRESS —

This is Lingo. She's a Dingo and she loves helping.
Anyone. Anytime. Anyhow.

It was a big day.

Lingo's friend, Sue, was off on a mission to the International Space Station. Departure was in one minute and Sue was running late.

"Look out for the banana skin!" cried Lingo.

"I'll be OK, but the mission is over," said Sue.

"I can help!" said Lingo.

But there were only thirty seconds to launch: hurry Lingo!

Quick as a shooting star, Lingo climbed up into the rocket.

"Don't forget this. It's a battery for the Space Station," said Sue.

The countdown began: Five, four...

Lingo buckled up.

3...

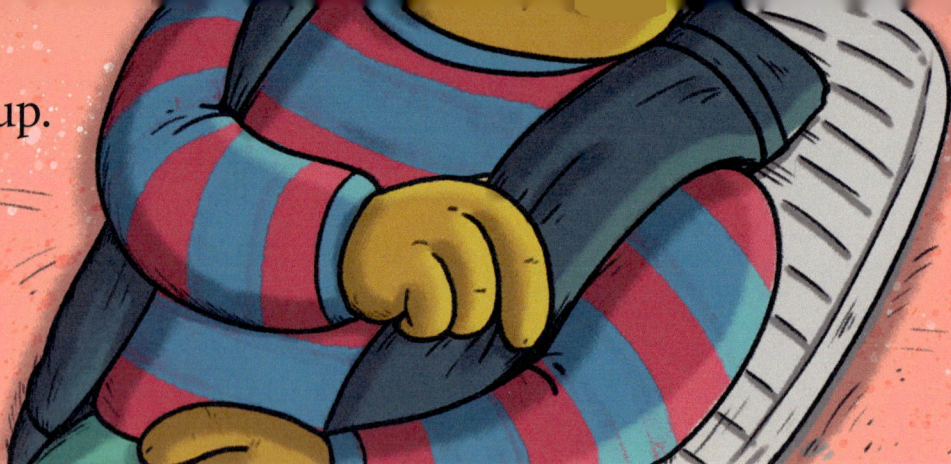

She felt nervous.

2...

1...

Blast off!

Lingo soon arrived at the International Space Station.

She was in space and she could f l o a t !

"Bienvenue!" said an astronaut. "Je m'appelle Rex. Je suis astronaute."
Lingo tried a reply in French, "Je m'appelle Lingo."

bienvenue = welcome; **je m'appelle** = my name is;
je suis astronaute = I am an astronaut

"Viens," said Rex. He led Lingo around the Space Station.

"Les toilettes."

"Le laboratoire."

"La chambre, et mon nounours."

viens = come; les toilettes = the toilet; le laboratoire = the laboratory;
la chambre = the bedroom; et mon nounours = and my teddybear

Suddenly a BEEPING blared out!

"As-tu la nouvelle batterie ?" asked Rex.

Lingo wasn't sure what 'batterie' meant. She checked her pockets!

as-tu la nouvelle batterie? = have you got the new battery?;
batterie = battery

A fishing rod?
Une canne à pêche ?
Non.

A camera?
Un appareil photo ?
Non.

This?
Oui, la batterie.

"Enfilons nos combinaisons spatiales !"

It was time to open the airlock.

une canne à pêche = a fishing rod; **non** = no; **un appareil photo** = a camera;
oui = yes; **enfilons nos combinaisons spatiales** = let's put on our space suits

"Tourne-la vers la gauche," said Rex, pointing to the handle.

Lingo turned it right. "Pas vers la droite, vers la gauche !" cried Rex. Lingo turned it left and the hatch swung open.

Tourne-la = turn it; **vers la droite** = to the right; **vers la gauche** = to the left

Space was waiting for them!
They got straight to work changing the battery.
"Passe-moi le tournevis, s'il te plaît," said Rex.

Lingo passed Rex the screwdriver and he screwed the new battery into place.

tournevis = screwdriver; **s'il te plaît** = please;
Passe-moi le tournevis, s'il te plaît = pass me the screwdriver please

"Mission accomplie !
Tape m'en cinq," he said.

Lingo realised Rex wanted
a high five.

Success!

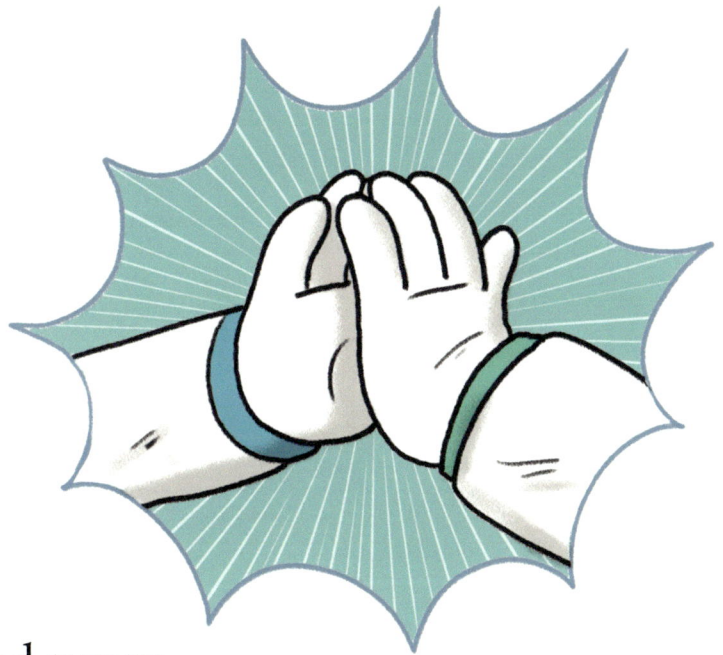

Lingo called Sue with the good news:

"We did it!"

"Yahoo!"

mission accomplie = mission accompllished;
tape m'en cinq = give me five

The view was incredible.

Rex pointed out all the things to see.

"Le soleil."

"La terre."

la terre = the Earth; le soleil = the sun

"La lune."

"Les étoiles."

"Le bras robotique."

But Lingo spotted something else ...

les étoiles = the stars; **la lune** = the moon; **le bras robotique** = the robotic arm

"Mon nounours !" cried Rex.

Rex's teddy must have floated out of the airlock.

"Utilise le bras robotique," he said.

Lingo was going to use the robotic arm.

mon nounours = my teddy; **utilise le bras robotique** = use the robotic arm

Rex called out the directions: "Vers le haut. Vers le bas. Presque. Attrape-le !!"

Lingo closed the hand...

but Teddy was too far away!

"Non ! Nounours est perdu," cried Rex.

"I can help," said Lingo.

She noticed something else floating nearby.

Her fishing rod!

She swung the hook out into space.

croisons les doigts = fingers crossed

"Croisons les doigts," said Rex.

The hook caught Teddy's bow tie!

"Mon ami," cheered Rex.
"Allons fêter ça !"

mon ami = my friend; **allons fêter ça** = let's party

Rex pressed a button and funky music boomed out.

Time to bust some zero gravity dance moves.

"Je danse, tu danses, nounours danse,
nous dansons," laughed Rex.

je danse = I dance; **tu danses** = you dance;
nounours danse = teddy dances; **nous dansons** = we dance

"Dis ouistiti !" said Rex,
and took a photo.

dis ouistiti = say marmoset (say cheese)

"As-tu soif ?" asked Rex. He squeezed big blobs of water over to Lingo. "C'est de l'eau," he said. "As-tu faim ?" asked Rex.

'Faim' must mean 'hungry' thought Lingo. "Yes," she replied. "Moi aussi," Rex agreed.

It was time for space ice cream: "Glace!" he said.

moi aussi = me too; **glace** = ice cream

Lingo and Rex snuggled into bed.
What an incredible day.

"J'adore l'espace," said Rex.
"Yes," agreed Lingo, "moi aussi."
"Dors bien, Lingo," said Rex.

j'adore l'espace = I love space

Lingo didn't have time to wonder
what 'dors bien' meant, she
was already fast asleep.

dors bien = sleep well

Learning to love languages

An additional language opens a child's mind, broadens their horizons and enriches their emotional life. Research has shown that the time between a child's birth and their sixth or seventh birthday is a "golden period" when they are most receptive to new languages. This is because they have an in-built ability to distinguish the sounds they hear and make sense of them. The Story-powered Language Learning Method taps into these natural abilities.

How the story-powered language learning method works

We create an emotionally engaging and funny story for children and adults to enjoy together, just like any other picture book. Studies show that social interaction, like enjoying a book together, is critical in language learning.

Through the story, we introduce a relatable character who speaks only in the new language. This helps build empathy and a positive attitude towards people who speak different languages. These are both important aspects in laying the foundations for lasting language acquisition in a child's life.

As the story progresses, the child naturally works with the characters to discover the meanings of a wide range of fun new words. Strategic use of humour ensures that this subconscious learning is rewarded with laughter; the child feels good and the first seeds of a lifelong love of languages are sown.

For more information and free learning resources visit www.neuwestendpress.com

You can learn more words and phrases with these hilarious, heartwarming stories from **NEU WESTEND PRESS**

LEARN 50 FRENCH WORDS

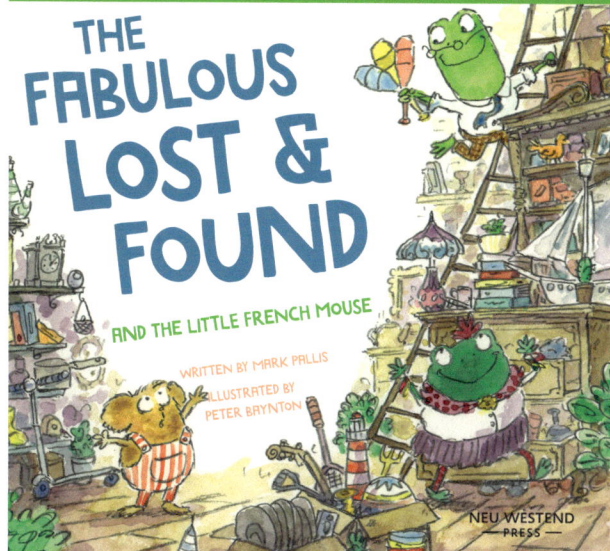

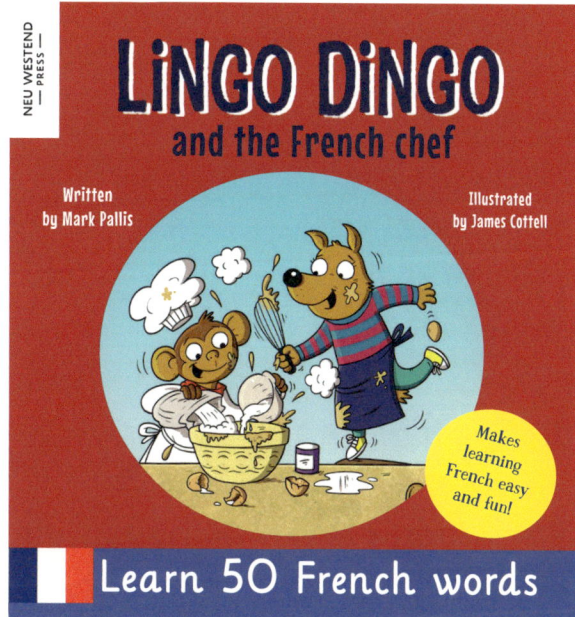

THE FABULOUS LOST & FOUND

AND THE LITTLE FRENCH MOUSE

WRITTEN BY MARK PALLIS
ILLUSTRATED BY PETER BAYNTON

NEU WESTEND PRESS

NEU WESTEND PRESS

LINGO DINGO
and the French chef

Written by Mark Pallis

Illustrated by James Cottell

Makes learning French easy and fun!

Learn 50 French words

CERTIFICATE

Dear _____

Congratulations

You are learning a new language.

You are a **star!**

With my best wishes

Lingo

NEU WESTEND PRESS

@MARK_PALLIS on twitter
www.markpallis.com

To download your FREE certifcate, and more cool stuff, visit
www.neuwestendpress.com

@jamescottell on INSTAGRAM
www.jamescottellstudios.co.uk

Crab and Whale is the bestselling story of how a little Crab helps a big Whale. It's carefully designed to help even the most energetic children find a moment of calm and focus. It also includes a special mindful breathing exercise and affirmation for children. Also available in French as 'Crabe et Baleine'.

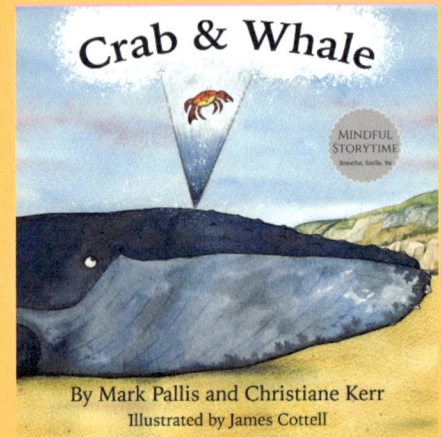

Featured on Mindful.org's '7 Mindful Children's books'.

Crab & Whale

MINDFUL STORYTIME
Breathe, Smile, Be.

By Mark Pallis and Christiane Kerr
Illustrated by James Cottell

Do you call them hugs or cuddles?

In this funny, heartwarming story, you will laugh out loud as two loveable gibbons try to figure out if a hug is better than a cuddle and, in the process, learn how to get along.

A perfect story for anyone who loves a hug (or a cuddle!)

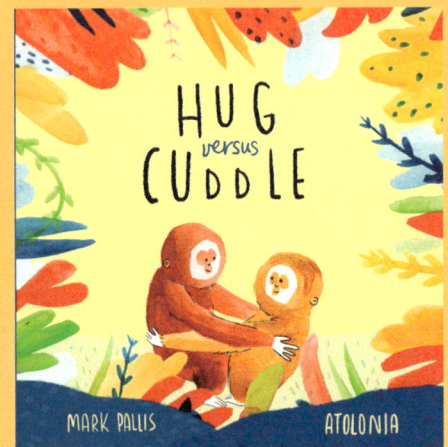

HUG versus CUDDLE

MARK PALLIS   ATOLONIA

www.markpallis.com

Made in the USA
Columbia, SC
05 December 2023